I0605894

IN THE CAPITAL CITY OF AUTUMN

Also by Tim Bowling

Fiction

The Bone Sharps
Downriver Drift
The Heavy Bear
The Marvels of Youth
The Paperboy's Winter
The Tinsmith

Literary Nonfiction

The Call of the Red-Winged Blackbird: Essays on the Common and Extraordinary
In the Suicide's Library: A Book Lover's Journey
The Lost Coast: Salmon, Memory and the Death of Wild Culture

Poetry

The Annotated Bee & Me
The Book Collector
Circa Nineteen Hundred and Grief
Darkness and Silence
The Dark Set: New Tenderman Poems
The Duende of Tetherball
Dying Scarlet
Fathom
Low Water Slack
The Memory Orchard
Selected Poems
Tenderman
The Thin Smoke of the Heart
The Witness Ghost

IN THE CAPITAL CITY OF AUTUMN

TIM BOWLING

Published by Buckrider Books
an imprint of Wolsak and Wynn Publishers
280 James Street North
Hamilton, ON L8R2L3
www.wolsakandwynn.ca

Editor: Paul Vermeersch | Copy editor: Ashley Hisson
Cover design: Peter Cocking
Cover image: emyerson/iStock
Interior design: Jennifer Rawlinson
Author photograph: Jacqueline Baker
Typeset in Minion Pro and Open Sans
Printed by Coach House Printing Company, Toronto, Canada

10 9 8 7 6 5 4 3 2 1

The publisher gratefully acknowledges the support of the Canada Council for the Arts and the Ontario Arts Council. We also acknowledge the financial support of the Government of Canada through the Canada Book Fund and the Government of Ontario through the Ontario Book Publishing Tax Credit and Ontario Creates.

Library and Archives Canada Cataloguing in Publication

Title: In the capital city of autumn / Tim Bowling.
Other titles: In the capital city of autumn (Compilation)
Names: Bowling, Tim, 1964- author.
Identifiers: Canadiana 20240321758 | ISBN 9781989496862 (softcover)
Subjects: LCGFT: Poetry.
Classification: LCC PS8553.O9044 I5 2024 | DDC C811/.54—dc23

for Theresa

with gratitude for thirty wonderful years

CONTENTS

PART ONE

PART TWO

PART THREE

PART FOUR

PART FIVE

PART ONE

Yesteryears

Took the fat family bible and tossed it
off the Lions Gate Bridge.
Goodbye Toronto pre-Depression infant death.
So long psalms of Edwardian fiscal failure.
Hurled it the same as Cobden-Sanderson
into the Thames his blocks of type
so no one could come after
so no one could traffick in his lonely fight
Good riddance to fleshpress and letterpress
the antiquarian appetites of every cast
let the orca swallow the bile anvil
for a fibrillating sponge
and sound so deep
I'll never hear the undertaker's step
up concrete walk to rented stoop
or smell the sighing midwife's sweat
as she wraps another swaddling corpse
in garlic breath and sentiment.
Limit the edition
to a run of naught.
Dropped it like a gargoyle cracked
by revolution off a parapet.
Dead weight of words and font
a typewriter not typed with
since the ceasefire of the Second War
engine block of a Molotoved car
who my people and their moments were
a ledger book of no account
to marauding tide and tireless neon
all the totems not yet poles
along the shore
one black eye for the sun –

no more to visit those dates
that everyone loses or keeps –
the cage with a dead shark
clamped to a dead limb
most impossible evacuation
the bone lifted from under the skin
future's twin.

Ancestry

My mother tells me I was baptised by no one and
nothing and all that ever touched my forehead
was the potato dust off the sacks of culls my father
chucked on the split linoleum for his winter bonus
or a few beads of bloodied brine he shook one summer
off his gillnet for a pittance. I do not beg
but I differ. The dandelion's floating sperm,
for one, broke dry on my brow all those years
I gathered the sacred waters off a dog's face
and knelt to marionette on creosoted planks
more than any god's patience. Understand –
I've thrown my childhood like a younger brother
into the pit long since and carry the jewel-less movement
of a grandfather's railroad watch in my mouth
to spit time redly into the rich dark
yet I don't forget the hush that fell on the river
when the blue herons bid me rise
and I parted the rushes and returned
to the meagre earnings of the earth and word
where there isn't any paradise for mother,
father, brother or son, and humbly we approach it.

In the Beginning

Between the bed where I slept each night
and the banks of a great river –
a girl I loved
and a vacant lot I loved.
Her attic bedroom looked out on
the fourth floor of the cherry blossom building.
I stood on the mezzanine of sun-glare
and dew, counting her heartbeats,
reliant on the seed-bent grass for touch.
If her face ever appeared
at the summons of my silent need
it is the reason I have aged
that the dew burnt off
that I held the sparrows of the pulse of life
in my hands until the feathers turned chill
and nobody carried the shards of the fairy-tale mirror
away from the place of decks and masts.
If I can see her face
can I feel the boyish impulse
to aspire to the rooftop of time
and survey – with the bald eagle's
circling gaze – the lineaments of hunger
that belonged to me and to the world
at once? Feel again – without thought?
I'm on new ground.
The river – out of sight – flows differently.
Whatever I understood of the heart's impermeable longing
lies deep under the dead grass.
Standing here, on the third floor of blossom,
in a dawn that more resembles dusk,
no walls, a single stairway up,
I can see her face

as old as mine
beautiful and growing cold
as the scales on the sides of the great plenty
the man I loved and would briefly become
tried over all birds' pulses forever to ferry home.

Encore

That night I broke my mental wrist.
My life hung like a dog's paw to shake.
But my kind masters were gone and going.
I felt the downward pull of that weight
on my wheel-bound shoulder only those
whose eyelids close nightly like butterfly
guillotines on manual labour can't help knowing.

Here is a street like any other. You can die on it.
You can stop and gossip with a neighbour.
You can walk a colicky baby to sleep.
Fifty years ago – pure vaudeville turn.
At one end, a small man in midnight streetlamp shine
dangling a forty-pound salmon under the gill
at his side. At the other end,
a small woman in a daylight rain shower
holding a twenty-pound bag of groceries.
Why don't they walk the distance between them?
Why does the weight of their mutual errand to survive
anchor them more than the night and the day?
The audience in the theatre – one man
with the blood of that fish on his hand, the taste
of that food on his tongue – can't even applaud.

It is the day of the long night I broke my mental wrist.
The streetlamp is the shivering sun
that scalds the flesh of the dead.
Human eyelids flutter over the blank of the salmon's black look.
The money in each of its red pounds
still pays my keep – to carry without acclaim
or recompense until the street melts to river
and the body to flow, to the spirit-morsel

all must eat at the feast of each absence.
The bone is broken and still must break.
Old couple, let me shift what you have carried –
cells and blood and flesh and rain –
into the sharp ache of my dull sleep.

Apprentice

Too cerebral for the docks
too heart-sleeved for the academy
I lit out for the west (like Huck)
to where the sockeye built
their great silver cliff in the Gulf –
straight over, one whole dec-
ade, alone but for the hearts
of the high school dropouts
who made me, I made friends
of only fathoms and salt, the one
saying "sink," the other "swallow,"
as two diseased lungs of the moon
breached without height to gasp
on sandbars sharp as human bone.
Washed back on every tide to town
I wore my mourning suit of rain
and plucked the black threads
of a typewriter whose carriage return
returned so far I couldn't recover
my time – always my footfalls
followed the orchard paths
whose blossoms had browned,
my hands pulled pits without flesh
from the bough – I had to sing
without voice on unread pages
while my tender makers sighed
over fire and stove
always easy in the restless now
of the uncomprehending love
with which they sheltered me.
The house thickened its shell.
Dead, the salmon pressed their

silent laughter to the cracked
linoleum. I struck and struck
each key each black and
gazeless eye from a creature
swimming too deep and fast
to touch or see – something –
a cutting wind off the clavicle bar
a cancer in the twinned carcass
of breath down there in the baseboard
dust of the derelict houses
where my youth married age
and carried solitude across the
threshold I sought to save
the life in the dead I heard
the knock in the salmon's
stilled heart even as my hands
in its guts were the boy's
hands who tried to hold
the pastels in place on the paper
borne home from the schoolroom
in the rain the open mouths
of the earth and the sea
the night's shell the silence
the ageless oils of time on my skin
the love with which they sheltered me.

Sweet Sixteen

The papier-mâché face and head
of a three-toed sloth
my daughter made
several years ago
has finally worked its way
to the discard bin
of adolescence. The animal
stares at me and I
stare back, too bone-
weary to get up from my easy
chair and start the chores
of the next phase of life
in which the modelling
of the exotic wild
succumbs to the postures
of the parameter self.
What's the big rush?
whispers the sloth
from across the room
under the marked heights
of the children
on the doorway jamb.
Why the infernal hurry?
Can't you see the distance
I've covered
in only a decade
without even a body?

Companion of the slow accretion
(time and blood, time in blood)
I feel the head and face
of who I was

one child's childhood ago
drift gently away
as if in search
of the kiss
that can never touch
those cheeks again
while my body
settles like wet sand
on the river bottom
to disperse with the tide.

Companion of change
who hasn't changed
enough to suffer
change
let us be the masks
of the drama
my daughter studies
and loves
so much still – the make-
believe
tragedy and comedy
frown and smile –
you, who cannot feel –
me, who feels
enough to swell a surplus heart –
which of us laughs
which of us cries
as the girl walks out of her room
fully in her body
and her years
and says, seeing where I look,
I'm almost sad to see him go.

The Family Portrait

My uncle who drank his family to ruin
who was called (to his face)
a little cocksucker by his older brother
(my gentle father)
whose compact size, speed
and nastiness on the lacrosse court
took him to a national title
and who, demented, ended
his days rearranging the fir needles
on the floor of a Gulf Island forest
in the off-season
coalesces to one redemptive image:
in a chair by a crackling fire
his shaky hand motionless
on his golden retriever's neck.

My other uncle who rarely drank
to excess and attended every
garage sale and police auction within
a fifty-mile radius
who saw the brains of two buddies
splattered over the bricks of Holland
and knew he had to live intensely
with a cavalier care for them
and who always played
the devil's advocate (blue eyes
twinkling as you spluttered your defence)
does not coalesce but expands,
rising from the smoke of war
with frames of dripping honey
and handshakes for all in his hands.

Two brothers, long dead,
who watch me each night
as I sleep
from a photograph taken
at some family function
in their young manhood
who sit laughing to either side
of the woman who gave them
life. Two brothers –
a dark eye and a bright –
who seem to ask
of me when I wake
to face the world: Are
you living for others
or only for yourself?

Yet why is the hand
in the golden fur
also in the honey and
why is one brother
rearranging his tears
to box up for the auctioneer
and why, woman
soothing the child's pain
and carrying the man's,
do we bid against ourselves
to possess what we can never own
the heat of that limited fire
the grace of that limitless debt?
Why does the blood stagger
so drunkenly through the ruins as it arranges itself to cry yes?

Demolition

I called to tell you that the house is gone
all the windowsills we leaned our elbows on
the floorboards that creaked with our mother's vigilance
the bedroom doors that couldn't lock the worn
spot on the hardwood where we lay in front of the TV
in the years before remote controls the humming
almost-human furnace in the furnace room
the mysterious vortex in the chimney – gone.
But without a widow for the widow's walk
why should it stay? There was no reason at all
for the house to continue without us,
our tears, sighs, laughter, the rare harsh word,
no need for the shadow of the great maple
in the front yard to cool our perspective on the street
or for the linoleum kitchen tiles to peel and trip
another unsuspecting guest – no reason.
Even this writing desk I saved to mark all change
where I wrote my early poems and will write my last
would be better broken and thrown to flame
for the failure of its surface to keep us whole
as we no longer sleepwalk without harm
or find fresh linen in the linen closet to solve
the nosebleed pillows and the adolescent dream.
I called to say that I'm cold and I want to touch the old walls
as if they were the flesh of our parents
but your voice when you answered told me
that you had already heard the footsteps
walking down the gravel driveway and the road
vanishing where everything vanishes
at the dark address of the street without a streetlamp
with a moonbeam like the skin under a wristwatch
in summer when the wristwatch is taken off
lighting the family passage to forgetfulness.

In Ladner Harbour

I went and sat by my father's old moorage spot.
My eyes of frayed stern-rope
my skin of planks
changing colour with the weather.
No boats passed
except the leaky vessel of childhood
that sinks a little lower
every time we look at it.
No fog, but the foghorn sounded
out where the fresh meets the brine
as a man cries (silently)
between the salt in his blood
and his mother's milk.
The river's handshake with the ocean
mine with Time
the clasp and unclasp
my father's grip
always firm
I can almost touch it
a branch in the fog.

Look long where I look:
the grey sky in the grey water
for miles
and the single nailhead of a risen seal
that holds the halves of the world
and a life together.

Education

The geese flying over the yard this morning
sound like the faulty school bell of the middle years
of my life. I don't think I'll go to first block.
My lunch of olive pits and lemon rinds can wait.
Inside me, always, the kid who can't see
the hopscotch squares for his tears.
But outside, too often, the polisher of apples
for power. The dog licks my dangled hand.
I think it's affection – it's probably salt
from the wiping clean of the boards of the world.
With the children gone, the house is a croft
burnt with the invisible fire of my longing
for their childhoods. School bell, church bell,
fire drill of the biological urgencies
that place us in the stony arms of banks.
If I could, I would do the long division
beyond these lengths we're given
but I'm falling behind in every class
except the one in the room that smells
of ripe blackberries and the grass
the grave keeper keeps, hearing the bell
in the bone of the pilots who fly the sky to its darker season.

PART TWO

The Great Gatsby Poems

(in which several minor characters from the novel and from Fitzgerald's life take centre stage)

I

University

Once I was younger than Gatsby and Nick.
Now I'm older than Wolfsheim.
My professors are all retired or dead.
I've sold most of those books –
Hamlin Garland's *Main-Travelled Roads*
and everything written by Sarah Orne Jewett.

But coming again to Fitzgerald's final page
fresh as one of his hero's beautiful shirts
I take off my glasses at my own funeral
and, wiping them, whisper, "The lucky son of a bitch."

II

The Trivial Actors

The novel's passionate . . . with such an abundance of feeling for the characters . . . that the most trivial of the actors are endowed with vitality.
– Gilbert Seldes

Ewing

Maybe because he was so shy
living in that mansion
like an albino bat
Fitzgerald gave him a flighty name
East Wing of the White House
some further if subconscious nod
to the listlessness of the republic
"I was asleep. That is, I'd been asleep."

Almost blind as a bat
in his shell-rimmed glasses
and trousers of nebulous hue
searching unhappily for Gatsby in the gloom
with the notes of Broadway hits
dripping like blood off his fingers
he moved on, helpless
without the rich, and his tennis shoes,
a trapped bat dragging one wing
across both Eggs to opulent Greenwich
– nevertheless today the most famous of all the Klipspringers!

Klipspringer

Everyone hates me because of those shoes.
Not fair. Tennis is hard on the arches
and I'm not the youngest boarder.
If that fellow, Carraway, had offered
me a pair of Florsheim's for the funeral –
no, even then I wouldn't have gone.
I stay with people, you see, and that means
staying until Death frees me,
or desperation – if a man can't roar
he should at least bed down with the lions.
Anyway, I wasn't the worst of the leeches
that summer – I never sucked the gin
straight out of his jugular. And if
you really stop and think about it
when I played for him and his girl
that day – badly, I was all out
of practise, I'm still out of prac –
It's either the piano or tennis
I'm afraid, no time for both,
even here in Connecticut –
I never saw two people so much in love.
To tell you the truth,
they rather made me sick.

The Butler with the Thumb, Ten Years Later

I might have resented the rich sport
who paid my paltry salary that summer
if not for all the citrus
fruits – hard to be bitter
with the scent of so much lemon and orange
always in the air. In the kitchen
the pulpless halves rising
like champagne bubbles
that never burst – I loved
standing out back among
the pyramidal heap of them
on my Sunday smoke break
gazing toward the Sound
the way I'd seen this fellow
Gatsby do once or twice
after his parties fizzled out.
I sometimes thought I was him,
leaning slightly forward,
my one foot tapping
to the beat of a silent
jazz number – some chance! – eventually
I'd flick my butts on
the juiced fruit, noting how
skull-like the rinds looked
in the ordinary daylight when
even the band had long gone
and the last leeching drunk
had ground his gears almost
to dust. Maybe I saw it coming.
Maybe I just saw my own fate
in that bootlegger's lonely stand.

Now I'm out of service
never lingering by citrus heaps
never getting any kind of break
just the bum's rush.
I hear the parties are dull
all over West Egg
since the Crash
especially parties
of one. Justice?

How like the dim headlight
of a death car
the moon is
swerving across the lane,
how like a worn thumb
pressing with monotonous purpose
to extract the bitter juice of the world.

Cub Reporter

Only a decade before "Golly-Gee-Whiz,
Mr. Kent" Jimmy Olsen at the Daily
Planet, an ambitious anonymous
cub showing laudable initiative on his day off
"arrived one morning at Gatsby's door
and asked him if he had anything to say."
All politeness, Gatsby demurred.
Apparently, there'd been talk
in the cub's office. He'd heard
a rumour about a swindle. Nick
laughed, gently put the kid off.
All the news that's fit to print
isn't actually fit at all. Take
the Mills-Hall murder case
of '22 – really, nothing was true
except the corpses and, of course,
they also stank. Fitz
borrowed heavily from press
accounts of the crime: two lovers
in an apple orchard – how romantic!
He also kept
voluminous clippings of his own exploits
and collaged like Eliot a forensic masterwork
of how-dunnit for the critics.

Kid, about this guy shot in his pool?
Kid, about this writer dead at forty-four?
Kid, about this Superman character?
Kid, this green light?
Kid, this Kryptonite?

Kid, no one cares what anyone did
unless they're rich or newly dead.
Get your ass out to West Egg fast.
Yeah, your big break.
Remember, kid, in Metropolis,
there's always another kid.

Boy with Brick

On the white steps an obscene word, scrawled by some boy with a piece of brick, stood out clearly in the moonlight, and I erased it, drawing my shoe raspingly along the stone.

In the brick's chalk
was the word *fuck*?
Yes, they had it then.
Or *cock*.
Fitzgerald often fretted
about the size of his.
Maybe the word was *American*?
He keeps a lot to himself, does Nick.
Fitzgerald used him like a piece of brick
to scrawl Gatsby in the moonlight,
an obscene dreamer
posturing on the lawn
of his ridiculous faux-Normandy home.

In the second and third drafts of this poem
I've changed *fuck*, *cock* and *American*.
I change them all again

drawing my pen raspingly along the stone.

Chapter One

Why did the narrator's dog run away?
Was Nick parsimonious with the food?
Too self-absorbed to give a pat?
Did the dog sense something readers don't?
Hell-bent for leather, tail between his legs,
running like yolk
between two cracked Eggs.

Girl at Nick's Office

In the typing pool so not his type.
My brother saw it straight off –
"You can't trust that high hat, Evie.
He ain't serious. He smells
more like a flower than a flower does."
I didn't care. Date enough fellas
and who wouldn't want a rose
to sniff and sigh at in the dark?
Funny that his name was Nick –
pure Greek, but he sure wasn't – and
those cheeks, they never knew
a razor's cut, always smooth
as a baby's tush – yeah,
I liked him. A girl just wants
to feel elegant after the end
of a sweaty shift tapping keys
and fitting paper like a corset
into place – even if it's only pretend,
big deal. Pal, I've had plenty
of the real. You can have it.
Like going to Jersey. That's plenty real.
I never should have gone.
That's when my brother saw his chance.
The bastard. It ain't like
his dumb Doras are the marrying
type. I know that type
cause deep down I am one.
My brother, he ought to
cast mean looks in his mirror
and leave me alone
with my sweet tall rose in this stinkin' garden.

III

Seldes

Although the reviewers of his time – except for Gilbert Seldes – did not recognize him as a great writer, other writers understood how important Fitzgerald's writing was.
– Matthew J. Bruccoli

Poor Scott? Sure, Hemingway
did the dirty on him
in print (as Hemingway would)
and the reading public
proved fickle (as it will)
and he couldn't count
on Zelda for much
by the end – even agent Ober,
feeling the Depression's pinch,
couldn't supply the advance
in perpetuity, and MGM's
lion was more likely to snore
at his script attempts. Still,
he had Seldes in his corner
(oh a Seldes for every author!)
whispering, "You've done it, champ.
You've got this big dope licked."
(This big dope being bland mortality.)
Seldes, who's only a footnote
now in the great biography
of the hack who cracked
up before he reached legendary status.
Seldes, the faithful critic
in the mercurial age
that's every age,

who knew for a dead cert
genius when he read it
and absolutely didn’t
have to know – for me,
who still writes, without
support, old sport, more than
a footnote. Seldes, Gilbert.

Fellow Writer Tourist, 2017

In Great Neck eating littleneck clams
with the pickled ghost of Lardner.
"You know me, Al. I'm Abe North
in *Tender Is the Nightcap.*"
Dead, he was still dying in his laugh.
Can't you hear it? It's the sound
of bathtub gin sliding down the drain
or a poor sap's footsteps echoing in
the empty rooms of his sacred vigil.
Maybe it's just these clamshells clacking
out their syncopated jazz like
some sidewalk monkey's cymbals.
Hey, Ring. Can a fella slake
his grave thirst with immaculate style?
Retinas, pupils, irises – what the hell
does it matter if you've got the feel
of the thing? "I died too young
and so did he. Stop worrying
the toothache that our lives were,
wilya? Slip me some panther sweat, Al.
There's only one way to make this grit a pearl."

Final Guest

Probably it was some final guest who had been away at the ends of the earth and didn't know that the party was over.

Beams of my headlights silky
as the shirts on his bed –
even when he lived, I knew he was dead.
Isn't that the point?
I'm just a reader who drove up here
from Bangor, Maine, or Bangladesh, or . . .
that's the experience of literature –
a great book's the lovers' lane
we drive to alone, making out
with the ineffable: wonder,
tragedy, loss of illusion, pain.
And Gatsby – he spooned only
with the self, the self's dream –
we drive up, he's still here
in his colossal mansion parked like a car
that's like a tuning fork struck upon a star –
who doesn't fall in love with
his own epic grandeur?

Kill the beams. Wait.
The party's not over
until we are.

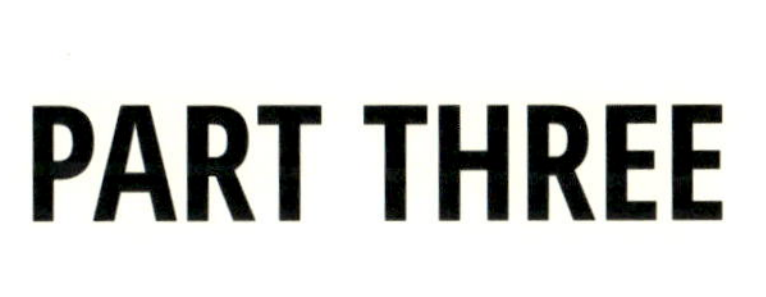

PART THREE

Cherry Blossoms

They were everywhere when I could be anywhere.
The weather of the world of wonder.
What else can be so beautiful before form?
Heavier than snowflakes, gathering like sleep
in the corners of windowsills, fooling
the sleeping spider in the wind.
The rusted wheelbarrow filled with pirate coin.
The windshield wipers wiping the perfume away all spring.
The barnacles on the black gumboots on the porch
when no one had been near the sea.
On the cashmere shoulders of the first girl I loved,
on her long brown hair, once on her mouth, and
distractedly brushed away, as I blinked
into the slow rain of the man I would become.
The man I am, more and more a memory of self.
The man who would pay to stand and watch
this parade without floats, without sound,
passing by the stillness of the unformed life.

Shopping in a Pandemic

Masked, distanced, fourth in line,
suddenly I see myself at the end of the long dark
of an open barn on a silt island in the Fraser River.
The air's rich with earth, brine and potato dust.
Two miles behind me, at my back, a pod
of orca breaches and sounds in silent
endlessly turned furrows. My father
helps the farmer hoist a burlap sack
of Yukon Gold into our trunk – barter
for the sockeye lying on the barn floor
staring wide-eyed as children at the rafters
several galaxies away. *Sir?*
How many hundreds of thousands of potatoes
in those great Aztec mounds down the black tunnel?
I think, they have eyes as the salmon have eyes.
But what is it they see now, out of their element
of earth and water? And what will I see? *Can* I see,
if I leave my father and enter the dark? One step
and the mountains tremble – the dead salmon
turn their terrified stares on me. A deep breath,
like a sliding under the surface of the sunlight. *Sir?*
The earth was so alive that I was growing from it.
The old Lab's shadow on the ground was a well
from which a man could draw his future and his past.
I started to walk over and have a look. Then
my father's voice, his raised hand with the key.
The world endlessly breaking in, *Sir, how would you like to pay?*

Men of a Certain Age and Cast of Mind

Men of a certain age and cast of mind
in gumboots thick as whale meat
in jackets of gallows shadow
their eyes the scorched ends
of campfire sticks seekers
of greater and greater solitude
yet whose hearts –
infant faces cupped and bathed
by young mothers –
cannot quite turn from their kind.
Men who exist in the world
as darkened lighthouses
throwing forlorn beams
on human cries
who tunnel through their cells
to find only more cells.
Men who have come to regard
their skeletons as fellow prisoners
on the hardened rondure
of the terraqueous earth.

Such men sometimes meet
their coffee black
their looks less so.

One washes like a fathom of salt swell
across a table.
The other takes his wave over the head
and shoulders, as a seal
takes the whole ocean,
rides it and makes reply
in his blinkless stare

Robinson Crusoe greeting Robinson Crusoe
without God's grace or succour
all the frippery of the world like froth
on some distant shore.

If you listen in
what you'll hear
is the raven's thought
seeking to unlock
the mussel shell
by dropping it
from a great height
onto bare rock.

Men of a certain age and cast of mind
whose knuckles abacus
their Book of Hours
whose footprints in the world –
multiple as gulls
over fresh gut –
shock no more no less
than the impossible emergence
of the same face in the morning's mirror.

Getting Wilder

The top of that pine tree
resembles a Mandarin temple
I visited once in the province of Bum-Luk
before those fools at the embassy
sent me to the frigid outpost of Na Na Na Na Hey Hey Hey
without so much as even a goodbye.

You can laugh. You don't know what it means
to be stared at by every crow
in a photographer's cloak
or to type every letter
through the thin ribbon
of a grandfather's manual
bloodwriter. That's right,
Blood. As in *Captain* starring Errol
Flynn who, too flabby for film,
and for what it's worth,
croaked in a hotel room
in the city of our birth
and all the dark drops of rain
left fingerprints at the scene
of the crime, which was murder
on the chambermaids, of course – passim

nor did he partake of the totemic salmon
swimming jerkily by, actors
on their own silver screens

this cut jumps like that, like life,

life jumps

like life

we hardly ever join one eyebrow to the other.

After Reading *King Lear* Again

"I have years on my back forty-eight."
– Kent, William Shakespeare

It's spring, the antiquarian bookseller's day off
from eccentric dust and endless
appraisals of worthless bibles –
we're all waiting
for the cast party for the cast
of *Waiting for Godot*
to get going. Spring. Just.
Fine ladies lift their skirts and stand
on chairs at the edges of cliffs
and shriek, "Eek! Eek! Lemmings!"

Spring – time to write odes to the ides.
I spy through my neighbour's open door
his wife blooming daffodils
in a sizzling pan;
over the rooftops
the Etch A Sketching waxwings
erase themselves and reappear;
in the valley, a coyote loosens
the cravat in a rabbit's throat;
on the sidewalk
a child I do not know
bids me, "Look at this, mister"
as if it's 1934, and I look
at the chalk beams of his architecture
as if it's 1664
and he's Sir Christopher Wren.
Just now, all the cabinet ministers

with their alliances to the sciences
cannot extract the wealth
from my eye-sands.

Spring –
The divorced parents *do* get back
together, the cancerous dog
uncancers and leaps – Spring –
we're putting vegetables
instead of men
into the stocks –
all of us, like the *a*
in *aria*, begin and
end and end and

Look on her, look, her lips
Look there, look there!

The sun
the lovely planet in his arms
goes down.

My Dinner with André the Giant

We talked of testosterone and concussion protocol,
power (drill bits a bit, boardrooms)
his hands cleaving the air's wake
like homeward hulls on wine-dark seas,
fame (his, natch) and death (also his).
He remains bemused by all the fuss
about *The Princess Bride*. ("It's
inconceivable, to say the least.")

A funny man, fine dinner guest,
each of his arms as wide
as my torso. I said, "About death . . ."
He nodded at the maître d'
and touched a napkin
to his tire-tread lips:
"Do you know the scene in *Frankenstein*
when Karloff as the monster
takes the flower from the little girl?"
I answered that I did, yes.
His smile made a still river on a planet
I'd circled all my life
but on which I'd never had to walk,
a world of muscle, flair and pain,
sweat the very colour of blood.
"I was the monster and the flower,
and both broke at the stalk."

Strange, we never once discussed wrestling.
We never even wrestled over the bill.
French to the last, he bowed
(like a count) before he faded (down for the count)
heavy as a tulip in the rain.

Poem Written on an Old Date Due Slip Fallen Out of a Book Borrowed from the University Library

after Issa

The world of overdue
is the world of overdue.
Oh and yet . . . and yet.

The Vegan Poet Atheist's Guide to Life in Alberta

Step one – move
Step two – if you can't move, move anyway
Step three – if you can't move anyway, hide

but with a child's pleasure, inside
a fort fashioned out of the cardboard container
for the new refrigerator – and old school,
with an *Archie* comic, a bag of chips, a transistor
radio and, later, a flashlight – only the Earth's
turning and the cry of owls to tell you the hours –
and when you emerge, a lifetime of flux and
learning and ideals ahead of you, come out
as the grizzly comes out of hibernation
into the world of male power, wary but unafraid,
on the hunt your own blood puts you on
wearing the grizzle that lines your grave
leaving a trail for the ghostly children to follow.

Report Card for Middle Age

Attitude	needs improvement
Hygiene	needs improvement
Working with Others	needs improvement
Attendance	intermittent
Penmanship	excellent
Effort	intermittent
Gross Motor Skills	holding
Leadership	non-existent
Canada Fitness Test	incomplete
RSPs	none
Pension/Benefits	none
Working Alone	exceeds expectations

OVERALL

X is likely to progress to old age, but it might prove a challenge to him if he doesn't improve in the areas of attitude, cooperation, hygiene and personal finance. He spends too much of his time alone and often chooses not to participate in group activities. At times, he doesn't appear to take his studies, or anything else, seriously, though he once produced an excellent flip-comic version of "Bartleby, the Scrivener." His penmanship continues to be top of the class, but as it is a skill no longer much in demand, and since X has no RSP savings and no pension or benefits, his later years could be very difficult. I would like to say that it's been a pleasure teaching him this past decade, but it has not been a pleasure at all, his willingness to serve as hall monitor between midnight and dawn notwithstanding. In fact, I fear for X's future. If he does not begin to apply himself, if his attitude does not improve, it is almost certain that he will wind up dead.

Neighbour Mirror

Eccentric? I'll say. He wore a human catheter
for memory. Ran blood from all his outside taps,
tears from all his inside. Grew only the cores
of apples on his trees. Birdwatched
for the gaps in flocks. I heard him sob
at an intersection once – an old man
who lived alone in a succession
of snowstorms, his hands still trembling
with the touches of the last dog he owned.
Now he's dead, as you'll be. I'll be.
The taps are rusted. The core-tree's
stumped. Same old tsunamis
of traffic. Eccentric? I'll say.

Found Poem of Strait of Georgia Insults

You're a Dull Oregon grape you black-bellied plover of a long-billed dowitcher. You lugworm you screw shell. What a walleye pollock of a kelp-encrusting bryozoan. Yeah, you heard me, you suborbicular kellyclam twelve-tentacled parasitic anemone. Your scaup's always been lesser, you three-spine stickleback spring-headed sea squirt. That's right, you hairy chiton, I said it. Don't give me any of your green falsejingle, you fat gaper. Who do you think you are, the Lord dwarf-venus himself? You're nothing but a flap-tip piddock with an aggregated nipple sponge. Come on, you pileworm you dubious dorid you squat lobster. You want a piece of me? Agh, you're all hollow green nori, you yellowleg pandalid. I wouldn't waste my time on a solitary tunicate like you. Yeah, so's your mother, you oblique yoldia. Goddamned mud shrimp. Surf scoter. Sea-clown triopha. Gribble. Sea noodle. Dunce cap limpet. Bladderclam. Whelk.

Story of the Nature Poet

"I don't like animals," the student
in the workshop said.
Someone tittered.
I smelled hot sun on earth
and fur. Water appeared
that might have been blood
at the base of my throat.
I couldn't sense my own face
in its bright perch above
my heart. In one tube
of the fluorescent light
a trapped insect scratched out
the letters of a word
possibly *love*,
more likely *hate*.
Compelled to speak
by age and occupation,
I had nothing to say.
Someone coughed.
The legs of a chair squeaked.
I had emerged like a coyote
from the depth of a coulee
to stand on the loose shoulder
in the rush-hour beams
or from a crater
onto the surface of the moon
in full violent earthlight.

What reason did I have to wait?

The student's
upturned fledgling face
her eyes pinning that strange map
of skin to the air –
how like a destiny it seemed
how like the birth of a world.

In the end
there was nothing
left for me to do
but what the animal does
in its extremity – lie down
in the merciless dusk and die.

New Diet

I don't read books of vegan ethics. No need.
I've seen animals in pain. My own face
in the mirror. Lifetime pass for that commute.
In my wallet – the temple-bruises the forceps left.
I always take them out to pay. Yesterday
I toured the exhibits at the zoo –
so much makeup on the pandas
and all of it dried blood. The snow leopard
looked so cold in the snow (with only his tiny spots)
I gave him my genesis bruises for cover. Today
I had to pawn the carcass of the only life I've ever lived –
a little beat up, the gloss all gone, one eyeball of mercy askew.
What do you expect? I've lived it
one terrifying Rorschach blot after another.

Cliché

At the end of the day
what if it isn't what it is?
Everything you were taught – corrupt
the god you believe in – false
all your aspirations – meaningless
who you always thought you were – wrong

Now it's the start of another day
and the long middle
and there isn't a television to hold your hand
or a Torah of pixels to study as you wait for the bus
nor the nomadic cry of your blood for a companion

when the day ends and the night begins
and there's no language to prop up your sleep
and your mind slips back into the sperm and the egg
and you have to think yourself alive using only thought . . .

as in the clothing store after the looting
when the clavicle bones of the hangers
shiver with life

and something new begins to walk across the broken glass.

3:00 a.m.

Night's middle. Mind's stuck.
Python swallow. Trying to put
a face to the name of a
truth. One cloud
dissolved by another
a passenger train passing
through twilight to dark.
Christ losing consciousness
on the cross.
I get up and go out.
Read the front page of the moon
until the print comes off
on my hands. Coyote's breath
the colour of the ribs
almost sticking through its fur.
I hear each pant break
like river ice.
Back in bed, on my back,
I set the tongue's trap
for thought, want
to kill what makes the hour
tick. Can't. Listen
as the panther's paws
erase the pawprints of the cage
of the elevator that rises
before the unpaid admission
and amusement of the mortal laws.

Geese in Formation

O uninspired tattoo of the less-than symbol
tiny above the planet as a daughter's barrette
frayed chevron of the officer of the end of summer love
I refuse to write the elegy you summon.

You yourself are never an ending
never collapse like the pinsetters' set-up
or vanish like the smudged pencil
of all my father's strikes and spares.

You are only creatures
with somewhere to go
called by the condition
of what you are.

– blood, not wings,
the basis of all
flight and
metaphor.

PART FOUR

At the Estuary

Am I dead? The blue herons don't lift off the banks
as I row past, the red-winged blackbirds
in the willow branches keep their bangles
hidden (as if miners' children
clenched one hot coal in their fists, the only warmth).
Not even the harbour seal is curious about me –
he slips like a gallows body
under the charred channel surface
and the intake of breath must be the moon's
newly risen in the twilight – it isn't mine.

So this is the mystery, then? To return,
as the salmon return, to the source
but without the salmon's will. I hold
the oars like a giant wishbone
and cannot make a wish – for what
does an aging man ask of his past
except that it be present? Soundlessly,
moorage, and the short walk up a steep gangway
in the fresh dark. The blood I slip on
is the blood in the sloughs of the self
I carry into the streets of childhood,
those bookmarks in a book forgotten
and dust-covered, the story
of small towns everywhere – a page
for the drunk, the bully, the easy lay,
the God-besotted, the dreamer,
the woman who weeps for all animal pain,
the clerk who steals from the till
his own pay, the unbeliever,
the florist who hides a thorn
in the centrepiece of the mayor's election,

the attendant at the pumps
who pumps his life into each vehicle
that drives away, the pinsetter
throttling the cold throat of the marionette,
the up-late artist augering holes of light
in the night's ebon parapet –
sentence fragments of a sentence
no Victorian novelist could complete.
I reach the top of my breath and wait.

Plate shift or boxcar shunt?
The town spreads a pure silence after.
I pull it on like a flannel that doesn't warm
and descend and drift, more smoke than a man,
aware of where I am not how or why.
These houses housed people I loved
or knew – it is so long ago
the watchers had to bow to the television sets
to turn them on, the acrid drift
from the ends of cigarettes formed
Grand Banks of fog – if you telephoned
for a friend or a doctor, in distress,
the ringtone went on and on and . . .
until you couldn't tell it from your pulse.
I feel that I am walking toward the receiver.
I feel that I will lift it like a bone from my own grave
and hear the shifting of swallows' wings
through the wires looped so low
with all the weight of human voices
the greater weight of their silences.
Listen. It is suddenly so late
all the programs on the wooden radios
vibrate with the live laughter
of an earlier time – a speaker
out of the dark wings knows something

about the hearts of men. What does he know? The truth?
I wish he would share it before I have to follow
the footsteps I left on this ground more water than ground.

Already I know what's out there
in the wet shadows of ocean at my back –
salmon like the tickertape for their own failed flight
the shredded birth certificates of the world.
I can hear the minds I never heard before
take me to my place I can feel the whale
the planet's shuddering elevator of sobs
descending to the cellar where crabs in khaki
portion out the human salt.

By the time I reach the gravel drive
leading to my parents' house
I see the red of the driftwood fire underlighting
the bough sagged with cherries
though it's so cold my breath breaks.
Arrived at last at the blurred address of loss
I have to bow under the spiderwebs
at the corner of the yard to save the spiders' work
as if to change the channel
on the television no one watches
until the end of watching.

Suddenly the channel changes.
I am at the gangway's top in twilight –
the same or another isn't clear.
Gulls the colour of breast milk drift
on a tide the colour of sperm,
the blood lacquering the planks
flows again in my veins.
Can this be death . . . so much like life . . .
that sleeping's a misstep

from gunwale to gunwale
and a long drop through a dark
that won't lift?
The blackbirds open their wings
the salmon open their flesh
the herons tear the selvedge of the sun
and reveal, beyond the fabric,
more water, more sun, more hunger.

Out there below all footfall
the undertow black with the choked breaths of suicides
the sodden stumps wearing their last green canopy
heavy as canvas the shorebirds whistling
for a shore they can't find
I turn the body of my life to the west
where twilight shivers on the clothesline,
but do not move, as the blue herons,
flying by the dozens to roost, dismantle the frames
around the still-wet watercolours of themselves.

In the Capital City of Autumn

In the capital city of autumn
streets glisten like the skin of windfall pear
and taxis languorous as drunken drones on the hive's lip
let off their fares at abandoned hotels
whose lobby doors close as they open.
I was born here.
The leaves fall, the sun sets, the tide ebbs . . .
Newsboys whisper day-old daily news
glassblowers are always out of breath
dogs are an hour away from being stray
and all the typewriter ribbons need changing.

In the capital city of autumn
the moon's an egg in the pocket of a running thief –
it trembles like the last tear in a child's eye before sleep.
I was that child, am that thief,
stealing what all my neighbours steal –
the hour hand on the town clock.
We always get caught
and write letters of apology with goose quill pens from prison
to the future that is already past
by the time our postal service of dray horses
and forgetful authors delivers the saddlebags of mail.
In any case, we're soon released
like goldfish from bowls that shatter in transit over bodies of water.

In the capital city of autumn
it is my job to remove the drab suits from scarecrows
and put them aside to dress the snowmen
we never manage to build, having no snow,
but our chief industry involves dusting the eyelashes
of the sad people in unframed oil portraits

and hand making the tape measures the tailors use
to outfit the anonymous lonely for their meeting
with the tall grass outside the home run fence of the ball diamond.

In the capital city of autumn
happy hour is more complex than you can imagine.
Together we all lift the needle off the dusty groove
of the spinning vinyl of the season
that defines us to the end of our days
which never end because in these blurred limits
there is no death only dying that begins at birth.
I was born here and they'll lay me at last
in the sun's sawdust where I'll wait for you
with the key to your apartment in the old octopus tank
of the aquarium we closed out of pity when the longing
in the tentacles became so obviously our own.

Welcome.

In the capital city of autumn
where the public square holds rallies for solitude
that no one attends
you're already a stranger to age and you're
growing kinder to yourself and to everyone else.
Here is your transit pass to the direction of the rain
and a journal in which to sketch the faces of the first people
to tie your shoes before their smiles dissolve to spiderwebs.

The fog's come. And two ship's masts in it
like the figures of my parents. I have to go.
Please return my life of tender purpose to its memory.

PART FIVE

The Old Communion

Wednesday to Thursday

The early morning after
the late night
the family dog, suddenly,
had to be euthanized
(the bleeding tumour
larger than any organ)
I picked up her leash –
dirty with November
mud – and pocketed
all the scraps of fur
I could gather off the carpets
and walked our walk
along the back alley down
into the valley of the river
as I let the fur go
impossible blossoms
from my unclenching hands
and the tears sank in
making my body so leaden
I had to stop,
the dowsing branch
no animal can retrieve
pointed straight back without motion
at the untenable current of my life.

Truth

We couldn't get the collar off the corpse.
Her lovely head slumped, our hands
at the stalk of the sunflower.
Gently, the vet tried to help.
But the halo had slipped and coarsened
to the neck. I cursed
under my breath. What good's
a keepsake if what's kept
is only pain? At last we loosened
the collar enough
to slip it off
and stand there with a rough
circle
two in love who had to sign our names
for her disposal
and a professional stranger
who'd seen this all before
and every day –
all over the city and world
in greater and lesser suffering
suffused in the dull sheen of loss
our dissolving human triangle.

New Commute

I was the only rider on the bus.
Then the driver got off.
In the terrible day
something straightened me like a tie
at the throat.
For a while, my hands are on this wheel.
It's getting dark and
I don't know the route.
Headlights in my eyes – acrid smoke.

Excuse me, driver, you keep missing my stop.

Statistics

More pets in the city
now than children
according to the latest census
but the world grants no allowance
for a grief like this.
I stood shaken before my class
speaking of the importance of metaphor
in poetry
but I wasn't anything else
(unless I lied
to myself and the young)

except the largest tear my mother ever cried
out of the blood and resilience of herself.

The Clock

My wife's late uncle
always had a dog
same breed same name.
As soon as one died, he got another.
Did his effort to forestall time –

I call and my own voice won't return.

Dog

Dog, you made me better,
brought me back to the old communion
and self, earth no longer so alien –
walking you, I walked on a planet.

Dog, you made me worse.
I wanted little to do with the human
world so bent on fear and death
and wore your love like a womb.

Dog, you have gone as you had to go,
and you left me like the birth
we never let you have, my future
better – much, much worse.

Supermoon

Never closer to the Earth in my lifetime.
At twilight, huge and golden
on the horizon. Heavy, warm –
I take it to my chest
as I took her in my arms
on the last journey.
Never closer to my life in my lifetime.

Returning Home

And so the dog Argos lay there,
covered with ticks. As soon as he was aware
of Odysseus, he wagged his tail and flattened his ears,
but he lacked the strength to get up and go to his master.
Odysseus wiped a tear away, turning aside
to keep the swineherd from seeing it.
– Homer, *The Odyssey*, Book 17
trans. Stephen Mitchell

Beggared as any man by the getting of necessities
of life, I'd pull up at the back gate
on my bike and she'd stare a long second
until my voice carried my flesh to her love.
Rising, the joy shaking from her body like sea water,
she'd splash me in a present I so often failed
to honour. What had I ever done
to deserve this resurrection of the child
I carried with so little ceremony to his grave?
Odysseus in rags, his voice borne to Argus,
the ancient hound he'd trained as a pup,
who lay on a dungheap sieged as Troy by years
and flattened his ears in recognition,
freed to die by his master's return.
Odysseus, home from the wars, covert
and cunning, unable to greet his dog
for fear of revealing himself –
twenty lines singing louder than the whole epic.

Who am I to anyone
who am I in my own sight
when I speak and she doesn't move
when I come home from the world
of ordinary whirlpools
and the rags fall away
and I stand like an open wound against the sky?
The joy's here. I'm awash in it, bone dry.

The Loneliest Number

That old band, Three Dog Night, named for an Arctic night
so cold you needed three dogs to keep you warm. And
for a life so cold, how many dogs? How many people?
How much fire in fellow being will take you, friend,
to the auroral light and galactic dark, emptiness
crashing against emptiness, the ocean lapping
its bowl without slaking its thirst, and your skin
tanned on the bone by knowledge? It's late.
Three dogs to the grave, one face to the frozen sun.

Election

Leaders could use more dogs and
dog-loss, let them carry
animal death each day
to the cabinet room, make
policy with that anchor
in their arms. I walk
today into the second week
all the doors of the flesh house
open, no secrets from the self.
Listen, there's a distance
from all affairs
where the earth
becomes the closing eye of love.

The Bark

For twelve days after she died
I didn't hear another dog bark.
I saw them – silent shades –
through plate glass,
dozens of them, various
breeds and sizes
walked by people
whose days still divide
into feedings, walks,
trips to stores for bags
of food, unearned affection.
For twelve days I heard nothing.
Even going out, alone,
passing the shades
passing the sun,
the most aggressive animal
noted my scent without a sound.
Had she asked her kind for tenderness?
I passed the sun. I pass it.
Just now, on my way to this life,
one bark from a fenced yard
indefinable by tone
not fear or hunger or pain
one bark out of the interstices of the world
one bark clear and naked
coldly touched my flesh
to draw me from my burden
to invite me to sensation
to wake me from my solitude
as she did

thirteen days ago
this day
cold nose on my wrist
one bark broke like the blade of a shovel
through frozen earth
into starlessness.

Space

Months later, her fur
on the Melton cloth coat
I rarely wear, filigrees of gold
on the body and sleeves,
my own grey hairs
on the collar: this loose
script seeking a language
blunt italics curling cursive
I stand on the threshold
of the house without an animal
losing all traces
(I could be the planet
shedding its wild) –
if I step out to face the day
the wind will do the work
of time and failing memory.

So still now, the elect
at the moment of ceremony
welded into a black robe
of hieroglyphics
with my own eyes on my eyes.
Slowly I lift one hair
(whether hers or mine
I cannot tell)
and with my cold hand
open the bay door to what's left of pain.

The Exit

Come into animal presence, the poet writes.
Reconnect and resurrect.
But when you enter, you must also leave.
I close the door on her bones and every text.

Ladle of a constellation in the cold black broth.
A valley away a coyote scents my rising breath.
I am my own animal in a human lair.

Come into any presence now
I blind even the hunter's eyes
below the scope.
I stalk my own heart.

Out here the stars
like baby teeth in a grave
never really disappear.

ACKNOWLEDGEMENTS

Several of these poems have previously appeared in the following publications:

The Fiddlehead ("The Family Portrait" and "Men of a Certain Age and Cast of Mind")
Grain ("Getting Wilder")
Corbel Press Contemporary Poetry Series ("The Exit")
The Malahat Review ("Found Poem of Strait of Georgia Insults" and "3:00 a.m.")
The Walrus ("Geese in Formation")
Event ("In Ladner Harbour" and "Education")
The New Quarterly ("Cherry Blossoms," "Shopping in a Pandemic" and "Encore")
CV2 ("Ancestry" and "New Diet")
Queen's Quarterly ("Sweet Sixteen")
The Best Canadian Poetry in English 2018 ("Found Poem of Strait of Georgia Insults")
The Best Canadian Poetry 2020 ("3:00 a.m.")

TIM BOWLING is the author of twenty-four works of fiction, non-fiction and poetry. He is the recipient of numerous honours, including two Edmonton Artists' Trust Fund Awards, five Alberta Book Awards, a Queen Elizabeth II Platinum Jubilee Medal, two Writers' Trust of Canada nominations, two Governor General's Award nominations and a Guggenheim Fellowship in recognition of his entire body of work.